Coaching
Unleashed

Set yourself free...

by Michel Lavoie PCC
(as related by Moka FCC)

Illustrated by Daniel Svatek

■ FriesenPress

Suite 300 - 990 Fort St
Victoria, BC, Canada, V8V 3K2
www.friesenpress.com

ISBN
978-1-4602-6865-0 (Paperback)
978-1-4602-6866-7 (eBook)

1. Self-Help

Distributed to the trade by The Ingram Book Company

Table of Contents

For our family: Danielle, Mélanie, Matthew, Philippe, Louka, Chloe, Charlie and Margot

With love. You are the best!

FOREWORD

My master, Michel Lavoie, PCC (Professional Certified Coach), was seventeen years old when he got his first coaching job—but I was not with him at the time; I teamed up with him much later in his life. As a young teenager, he coached a Little League baseball team and loved it. He explained the basics of the game to his players, motivated them, and encouraged them to think of themselves as winners. He talked about strategies, plays, and boosted team spirit. Many years later, he once again found himself in a coaching position, but the job description had changed quite a bit since those days back in the ball park. And I am here to tell you about it!

Allow me to introduce myself: Moka, FCC (Faithful Canine Companion). I've listened in on all the courses and clients in my master's life, his many years of formal study, and his close to 2,000 hours of professional coaching (in large part on the speaker phone). I sometimes think that I should have official coaching certification as well—but then again, the world may not be ready for a canine coach. So I have decided to publish instead.

I sat faithfully by the phone as he (and I!) attended his coaching courses, learning about the role of a professional coach. First and foremost, the coach considers his clients to be healthy and whole as they are. He isn't there to try to fix something that is broken or imperfect. Instead, he helps his clients find their own solutions—not merely by encouraging them, but by stimulating them to go forward, to get into action mode.

Along with him, I also discovered what a coach is *not*:

- *A coach is not a psychologist or a therapist* who delves into the past to reveal issues and facilitate healing.

- *A coach is not a consultant;* a consultant is more like an expert in a specialized field, one who shares knowledge and advice.

- *A coach is not a trainer;* a trainer shows people what to do and how to do it. That is not the job of a coach.

A coach is somewhat like an engineer who examines an existing structure to figure out what is missing and what is needed for it to be a complete success. In partnership with the client, the coach then helps set goals for success based on the *client's* vision.

Some people seek out a coach:

- to discover their values and their life's purpose

- to set goals

- to increase productivity

- to identify obstacles to personal and professional success and happiness

- to work through issues such as life balance, transitions, and career choices

- to develop leadership qualities

- because they feel overwhelmed

The coach provides the impetus that empowers the client and encourages him to bring forth inner aptitudes, qualities, and talents. Why isn't the client succeeding? What is missing? And what would it take to change that? The client is the specialist and possesses all the means needed to succeed; the coach ensures that the client uses them.

My master studied many different facets of life to be explored with his clients: the physical, social, professional, emotional, intellectual, financial, and spiritual. He learned that a coach does a lot of listening—as did I (phew!). He asks tons of questions and gives feedback. Most importantly, he makes powerful requests of his clients to push them out of their comfort zone so they can overcome obstacles and reach their goals. I often saw the coach resist the urge to offer solutions up front. A coach allows the client to figure out for themselves what they want and then helps them create an effective plan of action to produce results.

Overall, the job of a professional coach has always been about empowering clients to be the people (and pooches) they strive to be. I am so proud to have listened in on coaching sessions and witnessed the satisfaction, happiness, and success that so many clients have experienced. There's nothing like getting off leash!

In the following pages, I have sketched out the principal lessons I have learned by eavesdropping for more than twelve years as my master worked with his clients. Perhaps some of these lessons and experiences will resonate with you. This is not a treatise on the subject of coaching but more of a personal exercise book. Questions at the end of each chapter are for those readers who would like to coach themselves independently, or for coaches who are looking for a new approach.

Unhook that leash, enjoy the discovery—and please don't skip any assignments!

Moka FCC

* For simplicity's sake, I use the pronouns 'he' and 'him', but I am referring to all genders.

* * Names and facts have been altered to protect the confidential relationship the coach enjoys with his clients.

CHAPTER ONE:
The Big Picture

Note: If you are the kind of reader who skips introductions, allow me to introduce myself: I am Moka, FCC (Faithful Canine Companion) and I will be your guide from here on in!

Do you find life confusing sometimes? I know I do. From what I've heard, when my master/coach Michel is talking with clients, life can be confusing much of the time. But if I understand what I hear correctly, the coaching journey starts with determining what is important to each of us. Coaches call it "values clarification". Our values make us feel alive and energized; they're why we get up in the morning. They become our guides when we're in conflict, living in uncertainty, or in need of motivation. No one says that decisions are easy to make, but they're easier if we're clear about what's important to us. For example, I know that being fit and taking a walk twice a day is something I cannot live without. I understand that about myself. It's near the top of my values list—just after homemade puppy treats.

Let me tell you Melissa's story. She had a great job as a high-powered project manager in an IT firm. What could be better than this? Well, probably lots, because Melissa was not happy. She had stayed at home for twelve months after giving birth to a wonderful baby girl and had recently returned to work. After maternity leave, going back to the office was liberation from what Melissa felt was the constrictive world of stay-at-home life; it was a return to the world of competition and uncompromising professional expectations.

So what was the downside? Melissa felt guilty about leaving her baby at the daycare centre when she was at work. Who could possibly take care of her daughter as well as she could? And when she was at home, she felt she should be spending more time taking care of her professional obligations. Melissa was being pulled in two very opposite directions and was not in control of what was going on in her life.

Add this to the mix: Melissa's mother made her feel even guiltier about not staying at home with the baby and Melissa's confusion was starting to take its toll on her relationship with her husband. Becoming a mother had changed the dynamics of all of the relationships in Melissa's life.

WHY COACHING?

Melissa decided coaching could help her work out how to fulfill her desire to keep up to speed in the competitive professional world while satisfying her personal needs to be a good mother to her daughter and life partner to her husband. She knew she needed to find a way to get her work/life balance back on track.

LET'S GET STARTED

As the coach would say, "It's all about getting clear on our values." How? Start with the big picture and create a values hierarchy, which is really nothing more than writing down our values in a list, starting with the most important and ending with the least important. Take a look at the list below and start your own. The following are just a few suggestions of what may figure on your list:

Family and relationships
My self: mental, spiritual and physical health (walkies!)
Pleasure and lots of leisure time
Sports
Volunteering (helping others, community involvement)
Travel/discovery
Taking risks
Chasing squirrels
Learning/study—curiosity
Being an entrepreneur
Belly rubs
Money—earning/accumulating/investing/spending
Success and career

A good slipper to chew on
Being known/fame and celebrity
Creativity and the arts—writing, painting, sculpting, theatre, film, social media

Looking at our values is really the first step to getting in touch with what drives us, what satisfies us. Once the list is done, all our actions, decisions, and feelings become much clearer because we are more aware of the values that motivate us, consciously or even unconsciously. When we feel, just like Melissa, that external forces are controlling our lives, we are not clear on what we want and what is essential to us. We are floundering. Establishing our values (our internal guides) helps us get clarity in our decisions.

It doesn't mean that we control everything around us, but merely that we come from a truly clear sense of what is most important in our own lives.

Of course, according to the coach, our values and priorities evolve as our lives change and we go through transitions. What we liked best as puppies may be less important now that we are more mature. Transitions can often be a time of frustration, confusion, and stress. And Melissa realized she was living through a major transition. She was now a mother—a working mother who wanted a happy home *and* a career. She set to work with the coach on a list of values and priorities.

It took a quite a bit of honest probing and soul-searching. Ambition, recognition by her peers, monetary compensation and professional success had been important to Melissa before becoming a parent. How did they rate now in terms of importance? Was she really going to have to leave all of that behind?

RESULTS

After drawing up her list of values, Melissa came to understand that her most significant value was the well-being of her daughter and her relationship with her husband. They came first. By taking a meaningful look at her priorities, she was able to work out a plan with her employer to allow her to work part-time until her daughter was a bit older. This permitted her to spend more time at home being the mother she wanted to be while working and keeping up with the professional evolution of her industry. Clearly knowing her values, what was deeply important to her, and being confident in her decisions allowed Melissa to delay some professional gratification and advancement until her child would start pre-kindergarten. Delaying gratification was easier to do once she was sure of her priorities. It also allowed Melissa to be happier both at home and at work.

Less stress. Less confusion. Greater clarity.

Coaching helped Melissa establish a clear set of values and see her way positively to a more satisfying work/life balance. Taking it a step further, Melissa encouraged her husband to do the values exercise so they could both understand more clearly what was important to them as individuals and as a couple.

This is not the solution for everyone; this is one person's solution. There are no right and wrong answers—there are only answers that flow from an honest look at our values.

Now, where is that slipper?

SOMETHING TO CHEW ON

Establish your list of values. Remember, the most important value goes at the top of the list.

- _____

- _____

- _____

- _____

- _____

- _____

- _____

- _____

- _____

- _____

Now, reward yourself with a cookie!

CHAPTER TWO:
It's About Time!

Congratulations on creating your list of values in order of priority! Here's your next challenge: let's see if you can walk the talk.

As the coach would say (and he cannot say it often enough): our values are the source of our motivation. If we value something, we are motivated by it. If we do not value something, we are simply not motivated by it. Makes sense! If our time spent on what is important to us (career, relationships, personal development, spoiling our pets) is not aligned consciously or unconsciously with our hierarchy of values, we will always feel a degree of frustration and dissatisfaction. I know that if I do not get enough time chasing squirrels, I can get very testy. It's all about aligning our lifestyle with our values.

Sometimes, a value may not appear on your list in an area of life where additional motivation would be beneficial. For instance, if you are unhappy at work and notice that 'success in career' does not appear on your list, adding it may motivate you to adopt a more positive focus toward your career. Or again, if you now clearly understand that this is not important for you, you may decide to spend less time and energy on your career and more time on areas which correspond to your more important values. We've all heard of individuals quitting top jobs to begin a new life in a completely different field after making a conscious choice to do so. They are realigning their lives with their most important values.

Once we've prioritized our values, what comes next?

Bob's story is helpful. He had a great job working as a mechanical engineer in a top-rated firm. He spent fifty to sixty hours a week working hard to advance his career while making a good salary. He got along well with his boss and his team loved him. He had been happily married for seventeen years and was the father of three wonderful children. But much of the time, Bob experienced feelings of emptiness and dissatisfaction professionally. He felt guilty because he just couldn't figure out why he felt like this, given his happy family life, all his material possessions, and the success he enjoyed in his career. He faced a huge issue with his motivation at work.

WHY COACHING?

With some prodding by his best friend, Bob decided he could benefit from coaching to work out how he could get to the heart of his dissatisfaction. He was tired of scrambling on the mental gerbil wheel, having the same conversations with himself over and over again.

LET'S GET STARTED

According to many time management experts, we have about 110 hours of active time in a typical week. (Maybe just a little bit less for those of us who like to have a small snooze in the afternoon sun.) After Bob established his list of values, the coach asked him to look at how many hours a week he spent on his various values. Once he determined that, there were three questions for him to answer. The following questions posed to him are questions we can ask ourselves as well:

1. Based on my hierarchy of values, how much time do I spend on each one?

2. How much time do I *want* to spend on each value?

3. What changes will I make in the allocation of my time now that I am more aware of the importance of aligning my values and my actions?

Working with the coach helped Bob discover a certain incongruity between how he spent his time and his personal values. Contrary to what had fulfilled him ten to twelve years ago as he spent an enormous amount of time gaining expertise, building his career, and raising a young family, he discovered the value of giving back to his industry had now grown in importance. In fact, it had been quite low on his list until now. The idea of devoting more time to sharing his knowledge with others excited him. He realized this could provide him with the sense of fulfillment that he lacked in his professional life.

RESULTS

Mentoring and teaching became a field of interest and activity that increased in significance for Bob. He was inspired to share his experience and knowledge with younger colleagues on their way up the ladder. The question was, how would he fit this new activity into his already busy week? He began slowly by devoting one hour at the end of each day to meeting one-on-one with younger colleagues. When word got out, colleagues had to sign a waiting list to see him! This one hour became extremely valuable to the company and restored Bob's excitement about getting to the office. It did not take anything away from his valuable family time and got Bob back in sync with his time allocation and newly-repositioned value.

Bob's move wasn't as radical as quitting and starting all over again, but it provided a terrific new lease (not leash!) on life. He discovered the source of his dissatisfaction and, with coaching, was able to act upon it.

SOMETHING TO CHEW ON

Take your list now and write down how many hours you spend on each value in a typical week. How many hours a week do you spend on your top priority? On your second value? For example, if 'family and relationships' is your second most important value and you spend eight hours a week on it while you give twelve hours to community service (which is, say, number five on your list), you may feel some frustration, conflict, or incongruity in your life.

Write down an actual number beside each value on your list. This is extremely important as a concrete gesture. Take pen to paw and write it down!

Now it's time for walkies! You can get to work while I take the coach for a spin. I'm trying to encourage him to increase the number of hours for walkies on his own list of values. Our respective lists are somewhat incongruent on this value.

VALUE		HOURS

CHAPTER THREE:
To Keep or Not to Keep

Now it's time to go a little deeper. So far the assignments have been fairly easy. You should be comfortable with what we call your "core" values—values that are most important and influential in your life. And you are comfortable with the time you allocate to these values or are considering reallocating your time.

Here's a powerful thought: when we think of a value, our thoughts create an image of what we want, and we advance toward it; conversely, our thoughts can create an image of what we do not want, and we expend the same amount of energy trying to avoid it. The master calls this focusing on "values to treasure" and "values to trash". Obviously the values to treasure are the ones we want to keep and the values to trash are, well, the ones we want to avoid and eventually leave behind completely.

Take financial security, for example: We can advance toward being wealthy or we can avoid poverty. It is the same value of financial security expressed in different ways. When I focus on advancing toward being wealthy, I see wall-to-wall carpeting in the doghouse surrounded by hundreds of bones buried in the yard and am motivated to advance toward being rich. When I picture myself avoiding poverty, the image is one of absolutely no bones to gnaw on, not to speak of the lack of carpeting, and I am motivated to avoid being poor. The results of these two approaches are very different, but the energy we expend in focusing on them is the same.

Let me explain. Meet Joan, a single woman, for whom financial security was a principle core value. Was this value important to her because she wanted to create wealth or because she wanted to avoid something disastrous? She was often heard saying "I don't want to suffer from poverty like my parents!" Joan spent a lot of time worrying about keeping her head above water, despite a well-paying job and a prudent lifestyle. She became very proficient at stashing money away for a rainy day, perhaps to the detriment of her own immediate pleasure and happiness. Because financial security was an important value, Joan focused her thoughts on avoiding her parents' situation of poverty. But she continued to feel worried and insecure.

WHY COACHING?

Joan decided she could benefit from coaching in order to understand the stress she was experiencing around financial matters and to gain control of her situation rather than allowing the financial stress to control her.

LET'S GET STARTED

As my master says, focusing on what we don't want usually occurs because we have experienced a significant negative emotional experience around a value. As a result of this emotional trauma, a vicious circle is created. We think, *I'm on dangerous ground here; I'd better watch out.* What happens next? We focus constantly on avoiding the potential danger which causes our thoughts to create or attract more of it, especially when accompanied by strong emotions. As a child growing up, Joan lived with the fear of poverty on a daily basis.

With coaching, Joan examined *all* her values—not just financial security—dividing them into treasure and trash categories. It was a complete revelation. By focusing on avoiding poverty, she was attracting exactly what she did not want: a heightened fear of being poor. Joan was unable to enjoy her comfortable financial status as she continued to attract financial insecurity by focusing on it.

I listened as Joan worked on understanding that problems/stress/pain occur when we focus on a value that represents something we want to avoid (being ill, poor, unhappy), rather than something we want to seek out (health, wealth, and happiness). She worked at understanding that her parents' situation was not her own. Joan began to change her focus, concentrating on her own comfortable situation rather than that of her parents.

By changing her focus, Joan became aware of actions she could take to get what she wanted: untapped ideas and resources that could help her deal with her finances. New opportunities opened up. Perhaps she could make investments rather than leaving every cent in the bank. Why not take a course in finance to better understand how the world of money worked?

RESULTS

Leaving behind her financial insecurities transformed Joan's life. She took her first winter vacation in the Caribbean and learned that it did not destroy her bank balance.

By exchanging her fear of poverty for an inclination toward increasing her wealth, Joan was able to adopt a more realistic attitude about her financial status. She allowed herself the comfort of knowing she was secure. Her stress level was greatly reduced.

What we focus on is the secret of life. The mind interprets whatever we focus on as an instruction to create it and draw it to ourselves. And the more we are emotional about it, the more the mind interprets the instruction as being urgent. If you see people and pooches getting results, you can be sure they are focusing, consciously or unconsciously, on those results, giving their mind instructions to advance toward what they want. I was lucky to grow up with a belly full of warm milk and have been drawn to a full belly ever since. Focus!

SOMETHING TO CHEW ON

Take another look at your list of core values. Are there any values to trash? Draw a line through them. Eventually there should be no values to trash on the list at all—only treasures to keep. When you catch yourself focusing on what you don't want, use this opportunity to ask yourself, *What is it that I do want*? Then focus on the answer. Let the 'trash' value go. This may be one of your first steps toward leaving your comfort zone. It may take time, but the results are worth it!

When you clarify which values on your list are to be left behind, the coach and I guarantee you will experience important changes. Many of life's problems are solved when the impulse to focus on what we do *not* want is removed.

Tip: You can also carry a small note in your pocket or wallet with your new treasure value written on it to help change your focus. Eventually, you will do it automatically.

CHAPTER FOUR:
Whose Truth Is It?

The coach contends that normally, as children, we internalize ideas and beliefs from the adults, peers, and authority figures around us. These thoughts and beliefs then contribute to the image we create of ourselves, based on the various well-meaning 'experts' in our young lives. Parents, family members, teachers, other members of the litter, all have offered their opinions on our behaviour, and on us. They evaluated just about everything we did. When they smiled, we knew we had done something good, like learning to use the newspaper when we were being house trained; when they frowned . . . well, that was another story completely. Sometimes, we bought into their ideas and evaluations of us as the truth.

And so began the building of our identity and our comfort zone.

Telling you about the coach's client, Mark, will be helpful. Mark had a good job. The list of his achievements as he ascended the corporate ladder was long, his MBA and great personality having served him well. Then one day everything changed. He received a call from a head-hunter offering him a job which would increase his earnings handsomely. It was a dream career with the advantages he'd always sought: travel, bonuses, and an expense account. But after the call, Mark was depressed. The new job would require him to do a lot of public speaking to medium- and large-sized groups. *I have never been good at speaking in public,* he thought. *I feel foolish and I don't think that I look or sound credible; I don't like it when I have to speak to a lot of people. I feel very stressed and I know I'll blow it.*

He considered declining the offer because he believed he was not good enough. Others may not have agreed with him, but what was important and what motivated his decision-making process was what he believed about himself.

WHY COACHING?

Mark felt coaching could help him work on the influence of his beliefs and how they were holding him back.

LET'S GET STARTED

The coach often talks about how beliefs drive our behaviours, how they determine what we decide to undertake—or not. When beliefs are positive, they can act as motivation toward greater heights. When beliefs are negative or limiting, they can stop us in our tracks. And that is exactly where Mark found himself. It was more comfortable for him to continue believing that he did not speak well in public rather than to step out of his comfort zone and accept his dream job.

If our self-image is based on beliefs we have acquired from the various experiences in our lives, then we must ask ourselves these questions:

- What if our beliefs are misinterpretations of past events?
- What if we've been making decisions based on flawed information?
- How have these beliefs become our truth?

I've often heard the coach quote the amazing Henry Ford who once said: "He who thinks he can, can, and he who thinks he can't, can't." Such a powerful thought! If we once believed a teacher who told us we weren't gifted in creative writing, there is a good possibility that thirty years later we will still think we are not good at writing, and our behaviour will support that belief. This limiting belief will colour the way we see ourselves and make a huge difference in our ability to succeed at anything that involves the written word.

These limiting beliefs can snowball. If we once learned to believe that our peer group would ridicule us if we expressed any disagreement, imagine the power this belief would have on our behaviour as an adult, on what we would believe about communicating with our co-workers, staff, and more senior employees, as well as our thoughts about honesty in relationships. When I run with the pack, I believe I am free to say what I think. It doesn't mean I won't get the odd nip at my heels, but that doesn't change my belief.

However, being aware of the process by which our beliefs were acquired in our early years does not necessarily make it easy to change them. We cling strongly to our beliefs and will often fight to protect them. In fact, sometimes we act upon them even when it is against our own self-interest because we are comfortable with them. Letting them go may be too scary.

But these negative beliefs prevent us from seeing and enjoying all that is positive in our lives.

We are often unhappy, not because of the situation, but because of our *thoughts and beliefs* about the situation. But it is never too late to take stock and, more importantly, to take action. As adults, we now have the power to understand what these 'experts' were contributing to our self-image during our formative years. We can take responsibility for our own self-image and adopt new beliefs, our *own* beliefs that will ensure our happiness and success.

As others have said before us, "The past does not equal the future."

There is a lot to digest here—more than your average dog biscuit—so I had to go back and chat with the coach, asking him "What is the difference between *values* that motivate my actions and my *beliefs*?"

He explained it this way: A value is the worth or importance we give something. For example: "I value religious freedom," or "community service is very important to me." However, a belief is a conviction that something is true, even though it may be unproven or seem irrational e.g., believing that a four leaf clover is lucky, or that dogs make for a happier world—which is very true as far as I can tell!

Ideally, our beliefs evolve as we gain new awareness, as we become more conscious of who we are, and as we live new experiences personally and professionally.

The coach asked Mark what concrete steps could be taken to work on the belief that he was a poor public speaker. Together they devised a plan for Mark to take a public speaking course. When he felt he was ready, he began making presentations to small groups. He was nervous about his first appearance: speaking at his daughter's professional day at school. He accepted the request and plunged in. Many of the kids approached him after the speech to ask further questions. Mark couldn't have been happier. He was almost as proud of his achievement as was his daughter! Next stop: guest speaker at a local fund-raiser for a cause dear to his heart.

RESULTS

The main thing to understand is that we are *not* our beliefs. We *have* beliefs, but *we are not our beliefs*. Challenging our beliefs and the experiences we think support them is the first step toward discarding limiting beliefs. It is the beginning of adopting new and more empowering thoughts that support us to move toward the success we really want. It is not an exaggeration to say that the discarding of limiting beliefs is extremely liberating.

In coaching, Mark worked hard at understanding his beliefs created by past events in order to begin changing the present; once he understood them, he began to change. It was definitely a risk that required him to step outside of his comfort zone. Did he accept the job? Yes, he did, and he never looked back. His first professional public speaking event, which took massive effort (and not just a little perspiration), was the beginning of a long string of increasingly successful speeches.

All breakthroughs start with a change in beliefs.

One podium at a time! Behaviours do not change overnight, but the power of believing in oneself and knowing what is true for us is exhilarating. I know I feel that way every time I cross the threshold into the dog run.

SOMETHING TO CHEW ON

Beliefs are powerful, so discard those limiting thoughts and fly on the wings of positive beliefs that will take you where you want to go.

Take a look at these examples of limiting and disempowering negative beliefs:

- No matter what I try, I can never succeed.

- If I'm not successful by now, I'll never be a success.

- I am not lovable. People think I am the runt of the litter.

- It is better not to wish for too much—that way, I won't be disappointed.

- I could never succeed in a creative position.

These disempowering beliefs can be replaced with empowering beliefs such as:

- I will always find a way if I don't give up.

- There are no failures, only outcomes.

- I am happy as I am, the only multi-coloured pup in the family.

- I am responsible for my life because I have created my own reality (my favourite).

- Everything happens for a reason and a purpose that helps me.

- I can take credit for my achievements.

 List your top five beliefs about yourself.

_____

_____

_____

_____

_____

 What beliefs have had a positive impact on your life?

_____

_____

 What beliefs have had a negative impact on your life?

_____

_____

 What beliefs have had the biggest impact on your life so far?

_____

_____

🐾 Write down three positive statements about yourself—new positive beliefs you could add to your list to replace the negative ones.

_____

_____

_____

🐾 How could this new way of thinking make a difference?

_____

_____

🐾 When will you begin implementing your new belief system? Set a date.

_____

CHAPTER FIVE:
The Name of the Game Is . . .

What are you here for? What are you on Earth to accomplish? How will you make a difference? I hear my master ask his clients these questions on a regular basis. The questions are usually followed by a long period of silence. And from what I eventually hear, the answer is not always easy to find.

Now that we know what is important to us (values) and what we believe to be true about ourselves and our world (beliefs), where do we go from here? Purpose! Clear and simple. Purpose is what gives direction to our existence along with our values and our beliefs. They are all part of the same continuum. (The coach likes to use that word.)

Some say 'purpose' is a vocation, a mission, a life's work, but these terms all mean the same thing: our reason for being here. This is pretty big stuff. I know my purpose is to be loyal and affectionate to my master, to be his best friend and to protect him from any dangers I might perceive. I believe that a dog is man's best friend, so it follows that my purpose is to live out and act upon this belief.

Let's look at David's story. David grew up in a loving family. His mother was a nurse and his father ran the largest car dealership in town. From a young age, David, the eldest child of three, was respectful of his parents and did all he could to please them. He succeeded in school, both academically and socially. He was attracted to the arts and music in general. Like many adolescents, he taught himself the guitar and formed his own rock band. He also enjoyed acting as a mentor at the local kids' amateur theatre workshop. With college approaching, however, he had to focus on a career choice. Although he loved music, the arts, and all it represented, he eventually opted for the sciences in college—although he joined an amateur music group to keep a tenuous link to the arts and his creative side. He wasn't particularly happy about his studies, but something (family pressure?) kept telling him he should go into medicine. Finally, he did: he chose to become a child psychiatrist. Despite his success, ten years into the profession, David began resenting his work and the hospital environment. He wondered, *Is this all there is?* His professional life slowly went into a tailspin and he woke up one day in a state of burnout. What had happened?

WHY COACHING?

Apart from dealing with lots of rest and medical help, David thought coaching could help him get his life back on track—or, as the boss would say, "on purpose".

WHERE TO START?

In our very early years, we are taught to judge ourselves and others by external appearances e.g. "I want a lucrative career and a big house just like her." People aren't usually encouraged to focus on what will truly fulfill them. To do this, we have to go a little deeper, look inward. Purpose isn't something more to acquire, just another chew toy. It is who we really are, and that means our purpose arises from the values and beliefs that give meaning to our lives.

Once we are 'on purpose', we begin attracting results and true success beyond the material ones. We are 'in the zone' with ourselves.

As a coach, my master likes to explore an individual's purpose with him because everything that follows will be built on this foundation. This is an exhilarating quest! The coach encourages the client to probe more deeply into his own life. Occasionally, we see that an individual's purpose is clear very early in life, sometimes at five or six years of age. Unconsciously, a child may express his interior values; the seeds of a life calling are sown: "I want to be a teacher," "I want to build tall buildings," "I want to help sick animals get well." Ultimately, our calling is the expression of who we are. Once a client gets clarity about his own unique purpose in life, he will want to set his goals and make choices and decisions based on this discovery.

When we have found our purpose, we cannot ignore its calling. Who we *are* leads to what we *do*.

This is why purpose creates meaning in our lives. Without a clear direction, we may discover years later that we have been racing down the wrong path, barking up the wrong tree. To live on purpose is a great gift.

How can we discover our purpose? The coach asked David to think back to a time when he was totally consumed by something or somebody—when time did not exist, when he was totally absorbed in the moment. What peak experiences or special occasions in his past could he call to mind, times when he was completely lost in the moment, and felt the flow? What was happening inside? What was being fulfilled? What made him able to say, "This is me. This is where I belong. This is what I have to do"? David realized that his life at the hospital did not respond to these fundamental feelings of deep satisfaction. In fact, he hadn't felt anything close to euphoria since his early days of playing music.

"What is my life's work? What am I doing on Earth?" When people begin to tackle that fundamental question, they will have begun to formulate the words that will appear on their tombstone. Mine is ready: "Here lies Moka—a true and loyal friend."

Admittedly burnout is a pretty dramatic way of learning about oneself. David hit rock bottom in order to climb back up—and climb he did. David got in touch with his inner purpose. It's simple to say, but it can be hard work. (I know I have gnawed through many a bone of self-reflection on my own path to inner purpose.) The coach guided David through the process. He wasn't about to abandon his medical career, but he needed to find a way to incorporate more of what made him tick, what gave him that internal bubble of contentment.

What he wanted was to help children in a way that involved the arts, altruism being one of his core values. He looked at the choices in his life so far: had his decisions been aligned with his (newly-discovered) inner purpose? When it had been a question of theatre, music and the arts, or children, the answer was a resounding "yes". When he had opted for sciences and medicine as his career choice, he realized that his decision had been slightly "off purpose" or more in step perhaps with what external influences had in mind for him. Time to re-evaluate!

RESULTS

How did David benefit from coaching? He began to research ways that would allow him to remain on track with his purpose. He created a way to use music and theatre as therapeutic tools for children in psychological distress. He enrolled like-minded colleagues and set up the first unit of music and theatrical therapy for children in his city. As he saw positive results in the children under the hospital's care, his energy and sense of excitement were restored. Going to work each day was once again a joyful experience. This new way of contributing gave him the meaning that had been missing in his life. David had finally discovered his purpose, his ultimate drive and passion.

SOMETHING TO CHEW ON

Our purpose is the expression of who we are. Time to take pen to paw once again. It's important to write your answers down, not to merely answer the questions in your head. That's too easy!

🐾 What is your life's work? Your calling? What really matters to you?

_____

_____

🐾 How can your core values help you find your true purpose in life?

_____

_____

🐾 What is your greatest passion? What excites you the most?

_____

_____

🐾 Write down a time in your past when you felt such enjoyment that time did not exist.

_____

_____

🐾 How do others identify you? What do they seek you out for?

_____

_____

🐾 What have you been acknowledged for thus far?

_____

_____

🐾 If you had one year to live, what would you do?

_____

_____

🐾 What dreams of accomplishment do you have that will give your life meaning?

_____

_____

🐾 Who do you really want to be?

_____

_____

CHAPTER SIX:
Lights, Camera, Action!

Knowing what we want is sometimes harder than knowing what we don't want! But once we discover what we want, how do we achieve it?

David's experience helped us discover that our purpose is who we are and what we want to do in our lives. So by now we are familiar with our values, beliefs, and life's purpose as we grow and evolve. But what does this really mean? How do we get started on the road to self-fulfillment? How do we get on track with our purpose? The journey continues.

Of course, there are many techniques, but one of the oldest and most powerful—and one of the coach's favourites—is creative visualization. He calls it "focused fantasies" (this is my kind of exercise!) although it is by no means frivolous. Basically it means imagining ourselves being, doing, having whatever our purpose requires. It is like an out-of-body experience where we can see ourselves in the future achieving our purpose, like acting out the last scene in a film before the film is even scripted. It means seeing the images, hearing the sounds, and feeling the emotions of being in the flow *without* worrying about how to get there. We are in the moment, fulfilled. This is not magic; it is as concrete an exercise as writing down our values or beliefs.

Let's take a look at Margaret's story. Margaret had occupied various administrative assistant positions throughout her career although she knew she had the talent and ambition to be a successful manager. But every time she considered going for more, she heard her deceased father's voice: "Find a steady, secure job and stick to it. Don't take risks." For many years, she had listened to the voice in her head that had, in fact, kept her safe and comfortable, although it undermined her own purpose. Unable to allow herself to apply for a managerial position, Margaret watched as people her age, many of them friends, accepted more satisfying and increasingly lucrative career opportunities. This made her resentful and envious.

Eventually, the inner voice became so bothersome that Margaret finally admitted to herself that it was time to do something about it. Staying in her comfort zone wasn't keeping her comfortable anymore. Nor was playing it safe allowing her to live out her purpose. Margaret began to get in touch with what *she* wanted—the many dreams and plans that had been bottled up inside of her.

WHY COACHING?

Margaret knew that her purpose, what she wanted in life, was to be a good manager, to make things happen, and to create an environment in which she could inspire her colleagues to excel. But she had lacked the confidence to make it a reality. She wondered if coaching could help her realize the purpose she knew was right for her. She was ready to give it a try.

LET'S GET STARTED

As the coach would say, here comes the fun part—visualization. It is a powerful means of seeing what living on purpose is all about; it's like a dress rehearsal, a test run. So far, we've seen that one of the main keys to happiness and to getting where we want to go involves the art of focusing. So let's put some images to that focused thought.

Please be aware that this exercise can be life altering. Life altering! Once we begin to visualize and focus our thoughts, consciously and intentionally, we shine the spotlight on the results we want to create. Then we make it happen. This cannot be underestimated. How do you think I ended up with the best master in the world? (But don't tell him—it may go to his head!)

The coach likes to think that all human experience is stored in the brain like any digital data storage device. Margaret could choose to listen to her father's advice stored on her personal 'cloud' or create a new, more inspiring version of her own inner voice. To change her life, Margaret needed to reprogram her cloud, create new mental pathways. She needed to take old memories, advice, opinions, put them to rest, and replace them with new ones.

Why do successful athletes practice creative visualization? Because it works. And it starts at a young age. Have you ever been in the dressing room before a kids' hockey game? Basketball game? Soccer game? I have seen the coach's grandchildren practice creative visualization with their teammates before their hockey games. It is a fascinating pregame ritual. The boys and girls close their eyes, imagining major details of the upcoming game—the game plan suggested by the coach. They envision the sounds of the crowd, the feel of the ice under their newly-sharpened skates, the swish of the puck off their hockey sticks, the sight of the puck going into the opponent's net. They feel every thrust of their skates as their blades propel them down the ice. They feel the team spirit and how every player is there for them as they are there for their teammates. They accentuate the positive feelings of joy and winning together.

Visualization doesn't cost anything and it doesn't take much time. Ten or fifteen minutes a day, preferably at bedtime, is all the time we need. The technique is something like being a movie director, except when visualizing, we are both the director *and* the actor. We decide what we want; we decide what the movie is about and how we want it to end. (And we have the best seat in the house!)

The principle behind visualization? What we focus on is what we will create in reality. How can we create it and attain it if we cannot see it? What we think about will come about. The mind is that powerful.

Through coaching, Margaret began to visualize her life as she could live it:

I am seeing my ideal career happening in an old greystone building in an historical section of the city. The interior walls have been stripped down to expose the beautiful aging stone. I can feel the history. Skylights and large bay windows allow the light to stream in. The furnishings are modern and colourful. And my team, wow, what a team! Intelligent and dynamic individuals who are creative in what they do. Collaboration and positive feelings between the team members rule the day. I am comfortable and confident as a leader and our brainstorming sessions have led to wonderful projects that have helped us put the company on the map. Business is thriving, so I travel a lot; this permits me to visit many of the world's fascinating cities. I am happy.

Phew—now *that's* a vision!

At the beginning of the coaching mandate, my master asked Margaret to write herself a letter in point form describing what she wanted in the future for her relationships, finances, personal growth, health, career, and leisure, starting with the vision of her professional life. He then asked her to read the letter to herself daily for a couple of weeks before putting it away for a year. In a year, she was to re-read the letter to evaluate what had actually transpired. What Margaret will discover is that a lot, if not most, of what was written in that letter will have happened or will be a work in progress. This is not the stuff of fairy tales. Most high-level athletes use creative visualization because it works. Take a page from their book!

RESULTS

Creating and directing your life script is a very powerful act. (I love to think of myself as a director!) When we pause to think about it, most of us live on autopilot, automatically and unconsciously. We just cruise along without getting our hands on life's steering wheel. Perhaps most of what we have in our lives is based on a script we accepted many years ago—or a script written by someone else. With coaching, Margaret was awakened to new possibilities based on her own values, beliefs, and purpose. As the coach warned, "If you don't get behind the wheel, you'll be stuck in the passenger seat."

"I'll take those keys," replied Margaret.

One year later, Margaret was indeed leading her own team and getting fabulous results. She was working in a heritage building not unlike her visualization; however the furniture was not contemporary. (The real movie had a different artistic director.)

SOMETHING TO CHEW ON

- Visualize. Become the director and lead actor in your movie. Choose the scene you want. Make it about an event you sincerely want to make real. See yourself getting results. Make the movie as lifelike and meaningful as possible. What do you see, hear, smell, feel? Recreate this movie as often as possible, ideally just before you fall asleep and upon waking. With time, the new vision will replace previous visions and limiting beliefs. You will get the results you want.

- Master your positive beliefs; learn to use them consciously and intentionally and you will master what happens in your life.

- Be inventive and become curious about the beliefs of successful people. Check out their blogs, biographies, tweets. If they resonate with you as role models, experiment with their beliefs, try them on for size, and you'll also begin getting what you want in your life.

- Write yourself a letter outlining where you will be in a year: what will your personal, financial, professional, spiritual situation be? Read it every day for several days then put it away until a year has passed. Read it again in a year and the results will be clear!

CHAPTER SEVEN:
Get SMART

The coach refers to goals as landmarks on the way to making our vision a reality, the first steps to the attainment of the dreams we visualize. They're like a kick-start. (Some of us are rather more fortunate in that we have four legs which may help us reach our goals with greater alacrity, but that is for another discussion.) Now that we have seen the kind of person we are and want to be, and have seen where we want to go, it is time to create the stepping stones to getting there. And, more importantly, it is time to leave our comfort zone behind.

All our visions are accomplished through concrete steps or goals—small advances toward the desired outcome.

Let's take a look at Roger's story. Roger loved to run to keep fit and was happy in his accounting job at a medium-sized firm. He had not had a lot of success with finding the right life partner and had given up on that front. Roger had attended many self-improvement seminars and had invested a lot of money in retreats, introspective weekends, and a vast library of self-help books. In fact, he could probably have written one himself. He knew the theory and could discuss it for hours. Every New Year's, he traditionally established his new list of goals. Usually all of the goals he had set the previous year had been accomplished and he felt satisfied about his achievements. However, he noticed that this year his new list looked a lot like the old one, and the one before that. As usual, his goals seemed realistic. But were they too realistic, too easy? Were there areas in his life that he was avoiding that did not figure on his list? Was it time for a stretch?

WHY COACHING?

Roger wondered, *In what areas of my life am I playing it too safe?* After much indecision, he decided that coaching would help him find clarity and allow him to dare to go beyond his current expectations of himself.

LET'S GET STARTED

The coach starts from the vision, and moves with the client to square one on the game board. What steps will it take to get from 'Go' to attaining the vision itself?

Did Roger have difficulty in setting challenging goals? Did he believe he couldn't achieve them? Was Roger afraid of success? Or afraid of failure? Maybe he didn't think he deserved to succeed after all, so this was his way of making sure he didn't have to try too hard. Remember those limiting beliefs? Was it time to let them go and concentrate on the possibilities, time for Roger to think outside the box without limitations or self-censoring?

Being too 'realistic' can limit our choice of goals. We can think too small. Or we can avoid thinking about what may be fearful to us. (Just because I may be small of stature doesn't mean I can't run with the Labradors! Perhaps I should add that stretching goal to my list.)

Clear goals allow us to take the first steps toward the vision. As the master says, the steps need not be huge! Many coaches find the SMART method of goal-setting to be helpful. So let's take a look.

SMART is an acronym for a goal-setting blueprint. (Don't you love acronyms?) Goals should be:

Specific: Our goals should indicate as clearly as possible what we want to do.

> 🐾 Example: *I will run four times a week before breakfast* instead of *I will run more often.*

Measurable: Our goals should be quantifiable—how else will we know if we attain them?

> 🐾 Example: *I will run ten kilometres on each run* instead of *I will increase the distance of my runs.*

Actionable: Use action verbs, such as *build, write, contact.* Example: *I will 'heel' to my master on command* (not a goal I have as yet set, but a good example nonetheless) rather than *I will be more obedient.*

Realistic: It is important to know how to push ourselves just beyond our comfort zone—but with a dose of practicality.

☙ Example: *I will successfully pass all three of the Level Two dressage tests* rather than *I will qualify for the Olympic equestrian team.*

Timed: Every goal needs to have a deadline. By when are we going to accomplish this goal?

☙ *Example: I will ask my boss for a raise by December 31st* rather than *I will ask my boss for a raise.*

Roger worked with the coach to set up a SMART list of goals and a plan of action to help him move toward each one. You might be surprised at how powerful the simple act of writing down a goal or stating it aloud can be. But before starting, Roger was still skeptical, so the coach asked him a few questions to get him going:

What will you gain from achieving your goals?

What difference will this make in your life?

What will have to change in your thinking to help you get on the road to attaining your goals? What resources and people could help you stay the course until you attain the goal?

How does it feel to be committed to achieving these goals?

What can you do each day to help you keep your focus and motivation on what you want?

These were just the right questions to get him going. By examining his previous lists, Roger realized he was happy with his professional goals but was avoiding many personal challenges. He worked on being more aggressive with his running goals—why not the New York City Marathon? And the word *relationship* appeared on his list. It was time to acknowledge that this was missing from his life; it was time to add it to his list of goals. Why not begin to seriously network once again and get back in the game?

As I've heard many a time, big goals create full lives.

RESULTS

Roger was excited about working toward a new goal: finding a partner, a mate, a long-term relationship. Coaching helped him pinpoint what was missing in his life and gave him the tools to go after it. And the coach kept him accountable. Roger began to use the resources at hand: friends, social networking brunches, a dating service. He was not comfortable, but with time he grew to see that he was not alone in feeling this way and managed to acknowledge it with humour. The people he met were equally uncomfortable and it made a great starting point for conversation. Roger began to feel more confident and at ease socially with each small step. It was not easy, but definitely worth it. He began to stretch his socializing muscles and it felt good.

Roger also found a training partner to motivate him toward running the New York City Marathon. Putting his goals out there allowed friends and acquaintances to support him; this gave him a new feeling of satisfaction and motivation which had been missing from his life.

Psychologists tell us that people who achieve meaningful goals are happier than those who don't. So setting and reaching our goals *can* actually make us happier. Who wouldn't be encouraged by accomplishments and a warm rub behind the ears to celebrate?

Last seen, Roger was filing an application for his first half-marathon.

SOMETHING TO CHEW ON

Remember your vision. What do you really, *really* want for yourself, now? What do you want in your career, financial situation, your relationships, your leisure, your personal development, your community? These are now your goals. Take small steps; the only way to eat a wonderful meal is one bite at a time.

☙ Think about the coach's questions for Roger and write down your thoughts.

_____

_____

_____

☙ What would you go for if you knew you couldn't fail?

_____

_____

☙ What will you gain from achieving your goals?

_____

_____

☙ What difference will this make in your life?

_____

_____

🐾 What will have to change in your thinking to help you get on the road to attaining your goals?

_____

_____

🐾 What resources and people could help you stay the course until you attain your goals?

_____

_____

🐾 Reread your goals each day and make them real. Visualize. The key is to experience the feeling of attaining your goals at least once a day.

🐾 Believe. It is a deep source of motivation.

CHAPTER EIGHT:
Get Up and Go!

Now it's time to put our money where our mouth is. As we have seen, the coach works on the art of focusing. But without action, the power of focus is limited. Once a goal is set, the first and most important thing to do is to take immediate action daily—yes, daily. Even a small step will begin to move you forward. I have seen the coach's clients create small and even big miracles in the forty-eight hours after making the commitment to pursue their goals. Breaking down big actions into small manageable bites is what I like to call the "kibble process"—one small bite at a time.

Jackie's situation is probably typical. Of course, Jackie herself is unique, but you may be able to identify with her dilemma. A registered nurse in a large urban hospital, she had already established what was important to her (values) when she had attended a seminar a couple of years back. In order of importance, she had noted:

1. her relationship with her life partner

2. kids and family life

3. playing a new sport

4. advancing career

5. contributing to others.

Jackie had done some coaching after the seminar, but along the way had lost the energy to continue. It seemed there was no time to do it all, and somehow, her life wasn't playing out according to her plans. She worked close to forty-five hours a week at her job; her commute to pick up the kids after work took up another good chunk of time, not to mention homework, supper, and getting everyone to bed. Her relationship with her partner was difficult because they didn't seem to spend enough time together. Finding her purpose and visualizing was but a distant seminar memory. How could she possibly have time to work toward her goals? Jackie returned to work with her coach.

WHY COACHING?

Jackie knew coaching had helped her in the recent past, but she needed to reconnect with the process that had energized her and started her on the road to what she believed was her mission. She was currently parked on a side road going nowhere.

LET'S GET STARTED

Let's join Jackie in mid-coaching. She has written her goals but is not moving forward. It is clear that Jackie feels stymied, perhaps overwhelmed. Progress seems like just one more thing on the to-do list when she is already overloaded. But goals/intentions are just that until a plan of action allows us to move steadily toward them.

As the coach puts it, thinking and planning have their role, but nothing can replace action. Getting into action mode creates momentum and small advances. New insights and possibilities show up. Sometimes it's a case of two steps forward, one step back, but once in action we can see what is working and build on that. We can also see what is not working and refine our strategies. This is your action plan!

The boss feels that growing our network of contacts is one of the most important actions we can undertake. Networking is really about finding a mutual benefit for all involved. Helping others through referrals, articles, or contacts in an area of mutual interest can create a dynamic catalyst to move forward. (I know that information on local opportunities I have garnered from my canine connections during my grooming at the vet's has been more than beneficial.)

But coming right out and asking for someone's support may be difficult for many people. Fear of rejection or a straight-out refusal can stop us. However, asking for information, assistance, and support from others can propel us toward our goal. Some people will accept the request; some people will not. No need to judge; that's just the way it is. But if we don't step up to the plate, we've struck out before we've even begun!

One of Jackie's personal goals was to set up a regular night out with her husband every two weeks. Sounds simple enough. But she had to organize an evening when the kids had no sports, ballet, or music lessons, as well as when she and Michael (her husband) had no commitments and at a time when a regular babysitter would jump at the chance of a steady gig. Oh—and they had to *find* a babysitter! On the professional front, Jackie wanted to look at the possibility of becoming a head nurse in her current hospital or elsewhere. What were her qualifications? Did she need further education? Who could be a good resource for her? What positions were, in fact, available in her city?

Working with the coach, Jackie created her action plan. For each goal, she had written several small steps (I call it using the "puppy pace") so it finally seemed more doable when on paper. Jackie was ready to move forward.

However, at the following coaching session, Jackie still hadn't made the first step toward attaining any of her goals. After more exchanges, it became clear that Jackie was procrastinating because she was afraid that if she succeeded in reaching her goals, it would add more responsibilities and stress to an already busy life.

The coach asked her, "What will it take to get you in motion? What's missing? Who could provide more resources, more information? What are the risks involved?" After some silence, the coach pulled a powerful request out of his tool kit, and said, "Jackie, please take the first small step in the next twenty-four hours and report back."

RESULTS

Indeed, attaining goals requires effort. If our values, beliefs, and purpose motivate us to take action, it is only the action itself that creates results.

When we get into action mode, we are creating that all-important connection to results.

In the twenty-four hours following her coaching session, Jackie found a babysitter through a parent of her son's friend at school, then set up a meeting with the human resources department of her hospital before proudly texting the coach that she was moving forward. Jackie had moved into action mode. She began to feel the excitement of taking the first steps.

As agreed upon with the coach, she also reviewed her daily action plan and did at least one or two things every day to move closer to her goals. They were not always big steps, but each one gave her a sense of accomplishment and energized her to continue. Jackie did her research, met potential supporters, and set up a networking plan.

Working with the coach, Jackie realized that reaching her personal goal of a bi-weekly date night with her husband would actually be a great stress reliever, and going for a Head Nurse position was more than exhilarating if she actually allowed herself to enjoy the process, one step at a time.

We've all heard the age-old Chinese proverb, "A journey of a thousand miles begins with a single step." (Maybe they were into coaching, too.)

SOMETHING TO CHEW ON

🐾 One evening a week, on a regular basis, look at your agenda and write down, on each day of the week, one or two actions that you will take toward your goals. Do not leave any days blank. Be creative.

🐾 What gets you into action successfully?

_____

_____

🐾 Ask yourself what is holding you back from going for it and playing big. What is your first step to begin living without limits?

_____

_____

🐾 What does taking the first step mean?

_____

_____

🐾 As you take action, listen to the feedback you get from the people around you; use that feedback, refine your approach, and get into action again. Continue doing this until you've reached your goal.

CHAPTER NINE:
Life Re-tooled

As the coach has said, the coaching process is about creating change and transformation in our lives. Most of us are challenged by change, even though, strangely enough, it is one of life's constants. We can look at change as frightening—or as an exciting new opportunity. Take your pick. (Frankly, given my druthers, I'd go for the exciting new opportunity.)

However, moving through a transition phase can be difficult. Sometimes transitions are foisted upon us, and at other times the decision to change comes from us. In either case, the transiting itself can be a stressful experience. Do you remember leaving home and setting up your first apartment? How about moving to a new city? Getting married, a job promotion, a divorce, the loss of a job—all are transitions that confront people from time to time.

I've chosen one of life's biggest and most challenging transitions as an example: retirement. After a career spanning forty years in the academic world as an administrator, Kevin was on the verge of retirement, and he was fearful of what was to come. The working world had fulfilled both his professional and social needs between nine am and five pm. Of course, he had participated in retirement preparation courses, but it ended there, with little or no results except to make certain his finances were in order. He was divorced many years earlier, and though his relationship with his children was good, they lived in cities quite distant from his own. And, in principle, Kevin didn't want to rely on his children and grandchildren to fill his days. He lived alone and had been worrying about his departure from work for the eighteen months prior to his last day. He had been unable to act on what he knew was inevitable: what to do each day when he woke up and was no longer required at the office.

WHY COACHING?

Kevin realized he did not have the tools to deal with his situation. Intellectually, he knew he had to redefine himself.

But what was preventing him from planning for his new life when he would have to leave the office behind? Coaching seemed like a step in the right direction.

LET'S GET STARTED

In working with the coach, Kevin came to realize that the root cause of his immobilization was a fear of letting go of his professional life and identity. In fact, for all of us, fear is the most common obstacle to making a transition. Fear warns us that a potential risk may be coming our way and helps keep us safely in our comfort zones. When encountering real or perceived danger, letting fear stop us is a choice.

Much of Kevin's ego and self-worth was caught up in what he did at work—and he certainly had many accomplishments to be proud of—but he eventually came to understand that letting go was inevitable; he had to mourn the professional life he'd led.

Letting go is the absolute first step in making any transition. There is no moving forward without letting go of the present situation. As that famous person, Anonymous, once said: "You can't begin the next chapter of your life if you continue to read the old one." It sounds simple, but it's not. For example, it's difficult to get married if you stay at home with Mom and Dad. And in my own experience, I can attest to how leaving the kennel and my litter was very hard at first, but now my new life is fabulous! Whatever the situation—a project, a relationship, a job—there may be tremendous sadness involved in letting go. Alternatively, there can be great joy.

For Kevin, it was sadness.

He then advanced to the second step in living through a transition; this step is what the coach likes to call "muddling forward" (quite a professional term!). This is a time for trying out new ideas and activities; it's a time of excitement, of experimenting, of feeling a little lost; it's a time to test new hypotheses, and a time of questioning one's decisions—like test-driving a potential new car. This stage leads to the third and final stage of transiting: the freshly-minted you, the turning of the page to the creation of a new chapter in life. These stages apply to any and all of life's transitions.

But back to Kevin. With the coach's help, he reassessed his values as he muddled forward. The answers to the powerful questions "Who are you?" and "What is important to you *now?*" took priority over answering the typical cocktail-party-question, "And what do you *do?*"

What defined Kevin? What new ideas and activities did he value now? Was there anything stopping him from doing them? And most of all, what made him happy? What were his passions? He realized he had counted on the job to fill up his agenda, to provide structure and purpose to his life—as well as an identity—and now it was up to him to do so. It was time to become proactive rather than reactive. It was time to recreate and reassess his vision and purpose for this new stage in life. And the choices were endless.

In living though any transition, we are called upon to leave our comfort zone. We cannot advance to the next chapter without risks, large or small, and the challenges that accompany them. Nor can we grow into the new self with broader horizons without anxiety and perhaps some confusion. How rewarding it is to tame our fears, and to experiment with new directions! A new life begins just beyond the limits of our comfort zone.

RESULTS

Kevin realized that the more he took action, the easier it became. Not having a structured nine-to-five day allowed for fresh possibilities for personal growth as he muddled forward. He joined a local travel club and began meeting new acquaintances with similar tastes; he tried his hand at creating with watercolours; he had so-so results at first, but there was plenty of room for improvement! He adopted a dog (a great move!) which provided him with both a loyal new friend *and* a good reason to get out of the house; he even made a few acquaintances at the local dog run.

Kevin had always loved nature but had never acted on this interest, because he had had no time. Gardening at a local allotment became a new hobby, followed by the purchase of a camera to indulge in nature photography. The key was to take small puppy steps at the beginning, then medium ones, followed by even bigger steps.

Kevin turned a major change in his life into an exciting opportunity! For Kevin, it meant being able to say, "I am a gardener/photographer/painter; who are you?" Coaching is indeed about transformation.

Next step for Kevin: learning to play bridge.

SOMETHING TO CHEW ON

Retirement is only one of life's great transitions. But the three stages of moving through transitions apply to them all:

1. Let go.

2. Muddle forward.

3. Begin anew.

 What is your usual reaction to change? Is it fear? Does it excite you to provoke change? Do you prefer to let yourself be carried by events?

❖ What kinds of transitions have you experienced so far in your life?

_____

_____

❖ What strategies helped you in the 'muddling forward' stage?

_____

_____

❖ How did you feel once you succeeded in transiting to the new you?

_____

_____

❖ What activities give you the greatest pleasure?

_____

_____

❖ What obstacles are preventing you from moving forward?

_____

_____

🐾 When will you begin removing them?

_____

_____

🐾 What resources are at your disposal?

_____

_____

For those contemplating retirement, or for those who are already retired:

🐾 What are your strengths? When you were working, what were your greatest talents?

_____

_____

🐾 Describe the ideal week for yourself as a retired person. What are you doing? With whom?

_____

_____

CHAPTER TEN:
Who, Me?

The coach believes there is only one person responsible for the results we attain in our lives: us. *We* are responsible for everything we do; *we* are responsible for the good and the bad; *we* are accountable for our thoughts, feelings, the quality of our relationships and, in large part, the state of our health. The buck stops with us!

When things don't go our way, it's a lot easier to blame our parents, siblings, the cat down the street, teachers or circumstances in our past and present—and many do. (I'm reminded of the time the coach left that piece of chicken on the kitchen counter. Was it *my* fault I couldn't resist?)

Becoming aware that we are the only ones responsible for the way we feel and for the situations we are in is a big step toward taking control of our personal and professional lives. We are where we are because of decisions we have made, not because of our circumstances. If we are not responsible for our actions and our reactions, we have no control over the results. And so we have little satisfaction, little joy. Our successes belong not to us, but to someone else. If someone else is to blame for our failure, then someone else is to 'blame' for our success. (I would never let someone else take credit for my success on the agility course! I trained long and hard for it.)

Constantly blaming others for our difficulties has an enormous impact on our attitude as well. We become trapped in a negative mind-set. Complaining and blaming are negative energies and we are well aware now that what the mind focuses on is what it attracts: a downward spiral of negativity.

This is Andrea's story: Andrea was an entrepreneur with a catering business. She showed talent in the kitchen from the time she was a young child, and loved helping her mother and father put supper on the table. After graduating from culinary studies, she began *Simply Scintillating Suppers* as a one-woman operation, because earning her living creatively in the kitchen had always been her dream. Knowing firsthand what a busy time the supper hour could be, and how parents wanted to give their families healthy meals, Andrea found her initial market niche: she offered nutritiously-prepared meals as a "supper hour" caterer. Soon Andrea had four full-time employees as well as three part-timers. But the bottom line had been slipping for several months as her client list got shorter. She blamed the market, a recession on the horizon, the competition, the government, the high cost of supplies, difficult clients, or her employees who just didn't pull their weight.

Andrea suffered from constant headaches and had a knack for driving people away with her constant complaining and blaming. Not only was she losing clients, she was losing friends. "My competitor stole my best client." "My employees are not ambitious enough." "It is impossible to make money in this business!" The list of those responsible for her declining profits was endless.

WHY COACHING?

Andrea knew she had to do something. Her dream was slowly crumbling before her eyes. Nothing she had tried had worked. Something was missing in the way she ran her business and she wanted to figure out how to fix it.

LET'S GET STARTED

It was not the coach's first client with a difficult attitude when it came to understanding what had caused their predicament. Everyone else was responsible for Andrea's problems. But if she was not responsible for her situation, how could she expect to change it?

With her business slowly deteriorating, Andrea was in what the coach likes to call "problem mode". When we are stuck there, we cannot see our way to finding solutions. It is just easier to blame and complain. Becoming responsible leads to looking for true answers to our difficulties, which leads to real action.

Taking responsibility for what we can control eventually leads to solutions.

Of course, this doesn't happen overnight. We don't change from being victims of our circumstances to masters of our fate in the blink of an eye. Indeed, self-awareness and taking responsibility are among the most important personality traits of successful people. (We'll deal with self-awareness in another chapter!) Like most entrepreneurs, Andrea began as an artisan; she was brilliant in the kitchen. But as her vision and her business grew, she had to hire people to replace her in the preparation of the meals as she concentrated more on the marketing and administration of *Simply Scintillating Suppers*. But Andrea's employees in the kitchen were never good enough for her. She constantly meddled in their work and showed a clear lack of confidence toward them. She concluded it had to be their fault if business was declining.

Andrea looked at her leadership skills with the coach as well as her strengths and weaknesses as an entrepreneur. Most of all, it was time to leave blaming and complaining behind on the road to becoming responsible. Who was at the helm of this company anyway?

Coaching helped Andrea realize that her real strength was creating new ideas in the kitchen. She also loved marketing and putting her company 'out there'. She was great at cold calls, but her administrative skills were weak. And as far as inspiring her staff, she was failing miserably. Andrea's excuses and justifications for losing business needed to be replaced with responsibility and action.

One of the coach's questions hit home: "As owner of this company and leader of the team, what immediate action can you take to create more positive results?"

Owner of the company. Team leader. To someone who had started as a solo act, these were strong words. Andrea was now responsible for a business and seven employees. The need to step back and take a look at her entrepreneurial role was of primary importance.

Andrea was still operating on the belief that she had to appear to know everything all the time; if not, perhaps her employees would question her abilities, therefore reducing her effectiveness as a leader. Her first step, in all humility, was a decision to involve her staff: did they have any suggestions about how to turn things around? Turns out they did, and were more than eager to discuss new possibilities. After all, Andrea had hired them because of their talents, so why not take the time to listen?

Discussion centred on the fact that supper hour catering provided a fairly solid base, but why not venture into new markets to offset any ups and downs in the supper trade? How about desserts? How about creating new promotional events that would expand and build upon the *Simply Scintillating Suppers* brand? And was the storefront retail space necessary? What about social media strategies? And how about giving cooking classes? A new world of possibilities opened up for everyone.

RESULTS

Working with the coach, Andrea realized that being the owner of a business and responsible (there's that word again!) for the livelihood of several employees far exceeded the responsibilities of the former one-woman caterer. If her business was to turn around and get back on the road to success, it was Andrea and only Andrea who could lead the charge, but she could not do it alone. Getting out of problem mode and into solution mode became an exciting challenge. She began resisting the urge to do everything herself and learned what empowering her team could do to increase the bottom line.

Andrea also examined her responsibilities as she saw them. As she'd always had to do everything in order to run her company in its early days, she'd been trying miserably to administer the business as it expanded. She soon came to understand that successful entrepreneurs know their limits and do their best to fill in the gaps with talented people. Otherwise growth is just not possible. She made a new hire: someone to administer the company!

Andrea realized there was an alternative to being at the mercy of the circumstances of her business, of blaming the market, the competition, the clients. Her big breakthrough came when she understood that she had options. Instead of living in response to her circumstances, she could take a stand, become responsible and take action. She went from problem mode to active solution mode.

Andrea not only owned her company—she now owned her actions and successes. And, for the record, her headaches disappeared.

We may not be able to control every circumstance, but we can be responsible for our responses to them and begin to create the results we want.

SOMETHING TO CHEW ON

What does taking 100% responsibility for your life mean to you?

_____

_____

❖ In what areas of your personal or professional life would you like to become more responsible?

_____

_____

❖ What actions can you take to assume these new responsibilities?

_____

_____

❖ How do you think this will make you feel?

_____

_____

❖ When will you do this?

_____

_____

CHAPTER ELEVEN:
What If . . . ?

Time to have some fun! So in the name of my master, I challenge you to ask yourself some of the powerful questions you will discover in this chapter. Good coaches ask good questions. Masterful coaches, like my coach, ask powerful questions. But first, a little background to get you started.

As we know, questions can be used to get information, to clarify a situation, to help someone discover new insights, to encourage someone to act. Indeed, questions are an invitation to think and feel! That's what makes us human (and, of course, canine).

Martin's situation can shed some light on this idea of powerful questions—and help you to ask your own. He was a regional director of a newly-merged television/online broadcaster. Martin loved his colleagues, the responsibilities, and the successes he'd had in the previous three years retooling the business in line with evolving technologies. But getting to this point hadn't been easy. He'd had to deal with forceful unions, move 'dead wood' to more appropriate locations, work with creative producers, increase financing and trim budgets. His relationship with his wife, Janet, had been neglected as a result of the stress and long hours spent at the office. It had been trying on his health as well, but all seemed to be running smoothly now. Martin could finally reap the rewards of his hard work and breathe a little more easily. And then, in a surprising turn of events, his boss announced with great fanfare that the company wanted to promote him to headquarters to take on even bigger challenges. He was taken aback. After calling his wife to share this unexpected offer, he called the coach.

WHY COACHING?

This was both difficult and exciting news for Martin. Just as his life was finally rolling along at a more human pace, a wrench had been tossed into the works and he needed to figure out a game plan. And what of his wife's career path?

How did that figure into the mix? There were many advantages to moving ahead—and disadvantages as well. He turned to coaching to work it through.

LET'S GET STARTED

Let's look at how the questions we ask ourselves lead to answers and solutions in our lives.

We know that powerful questions help us to look at ourselves.

What do I want?

What are my options going forward?

How can I have more fun?

How can I play even bigger?

What is my passion?

The coach listened very carefully as Martin described his situation. What were the key words he used? Did they involve his values? Was he living according to his priorities, or those of the company? Was he on purpose? What gave him a sense of joy? And, of course, the all-powerful question: If money were no object, what would you do?

Over a few sessions, the coach asked Martin many open-ended questions. As he worked on his responses to these questions, Martin considered many possibilities situated just 'outside the box', particularly his answers to:

Where am I really heading at the moment?

What can I learn from this situation in order to move toward what I want?

What will happen if I accept the offer?

What will happen I do *not* accept the offer?

These are questions that lead directly to producing concrete decisions and results instead of just replaying those interior conversations we all have with ourselves. (I call them "chasing your tail conversations"—the perfect way to stay stuck in the problem rather than finding real creative solutions.)

Martin experienced a breakthrough when he realized that, for him, this was all about 'being' rather than 'having'. It was about more money, head office, greater status versus the status quo. Was having more money and more status higher on his list of values than what his current situation offered? Working with the coach, he recognized that it was really about who he wanted to be and where he could best be that person. And how could his decision align with the needs of his life partner? Where could she be the person she wanted to be? The couple spent a few evenings together exploring the possibilities.

RESULTS

Martin decided not to accept the offer. His wife and family topped the list of his values and he hadn't had a lot of time recently to spend with them. His kids seemed to be growing at the speed of light. He didn't want to miss any more time with them than was absolutely necessary. His wife had a job she really enjoyed, and perhaps this wasn't the best time for her to walk away from it. At age forty, Martin realized that he still had plenty of time to eventually go for a promotion with his current employer or perhaps with another company at a later date.

Yes, there was money and status involved in the new job, but the challenges and opportunities of his current position still allowed him to use his talents and be the successful person he thought he could be, both personally and professionally.

SOMETHING TO CHEW ON

Use these powerful questions to guide yourself, to open new horizons. Notice there are no 'yes' or 'no' answers:

How can I describe where I am at presently?

_____

_____

What do I really want?

_____

_____

What are the possibilities for me?

_____

_____

What area(s) of my life do I want most to advance in?

_____

_____

What's important for me at this stage?

_____

_____

🐾 What's next?

_____

_____

🐾 What are the wild options—the ones that scare me?

_____

_____

🐾 How can I make this fun?

_____

_____

CHAPTER TWELVE:
Baggage Check

When travelling, the more baggage we pack and drag behind us, the harder it is to carry it all. (I know I tend to pack way too much as there are certain chew toys that I just cannot leave behind!)

But we're talking about a different kind of baggage here, baggage that stops us from moving forward. And as the coach is known to say: "You have two options: let go or be stuck in place." It may sound a little blunt, but that's the way it is.

It may mean letting go of a number of things: a person, a past event, a fear, a limiting belief or a troubling situation. It may involve becoming responsible and not remaining a victim. It may even involve forgiveness. But as I have heard during many coaching sessions, the important thing to realize is that letting go does not mean surrendering or giving up. Giving up and letting go are *not* synonymous. Letting go allows us to move forward to a new space whereas giving up keeps us stuck.

Letting go is not only a proactive measure but an amazing way of gaining a new perspective on our lives. The joy that I've seen the coach experience as his clients feel the liberation of letting go is incomparable.

Here's a tough situation: Diane lost her job as part of the sales team in a medium-sized corporation. It wasn't the result of a 'right-sizing' operation. She was let go. Period. It was a brutal time. Even the severance pay didn't compensate for Diane's anger, sadness, and emotional turmoil. She felt bruised and battered after several months of a difficult relationship which began when the new team leader came on board. Life was terrific before the former sales team leader left the company for greener pastures. Everything seemed to go downhill after his departure. Diane was unable to connect with the new hire and felt her performance would never be acceptable to, let alone appreciated by, her new boss.

She was now back on the job market, but selling herself was like climbing Mount Everest. On the advice of a friend, Diane called the coach.

WHY COACHING?

Diane's confidence was completely shaken and she could not seem to get in touch with her previous successful and positive attitude—the all-important aspect of being in sales! People want to buy from winners. She couldn't stop asking "Why me? Why not somebody else? Why did it happen? Why now?" She was constantly looking for a reason, an explanation or justification for having lost her job.

LET'S GET STARTED!

We often get stuck in 'why' mode. It is easier, of course, to try to analyze the situation, to find an answer to the disappointment. *Why did my relationship fall apart? Why didn't I get the promotion?* It allows us to stay in the world of facts: *My boy/girlfriend will never be faithful. No one likes the new boss.* By looking for reasons and excuses, we can avoid more difficult personal feelings such as rejection, worthlessness, or fear of being incompetent or unlovable. But when the answers to the 'why' questions are out of our control, it is time to let go and move on.

What is the point of going over a situation again and again if we are unable to have any influence on it whatsoever? Finding new reasons or causes to justify what happened is not going to make it un-happen. Of course, we can benefit from analyzing the situation for future reference, but it is more constructive to deal with how to move on. That's where the coach comes in.

Yes, it sounds easy. But letting go in order to move on can be a painful process.

Knowing that sometimes people just need to vent before moving on, the coach explored Diane's emotions with her; what were her true feelings around the job loss? Up came the powerful questions: How does asking 'why' or looking for explanations help you avoid what you are truly feeling? How does it help you move forward? (you guessed it—it doesn't!) 'Why' has never been a powerful coaching question. So the coach asked, "What benefit is holding on to this past event allowing you? What could happen and what would it feel like if you chose to let go of the thoughts surrounding what happened with your boss? How could you turn the situation around immediately to regain peace of mind? What is the best way to let go of this pain-generating event? What's the next step?"

Phew. Tough questions. While considering these last questions, Diane arrived at the conclusion that she could continue to resist the situation, or simply let it go and begin to change her attitude. As Carl Jung is quoted as saying, "What we resist persists." There's no need to empower what is stopping us from moving on!

But coaching, as I have mentioned, is not therapy. The coach's task is to help us move toward what we want and, in this case, to release what doesn't help us move forward. So the coach asked Diane to list her top five strengths, a standard coaching tool. Next, Diane worked on writing an action plan to look at how she could concretely use each strength/talent to move forward.

Just getting in touch with her strengths was empowering. When we begin to take action, the door to letting go opens. Taking action gets us unstuck! Diane slowly began to ask 'why' less often.

And then the coach asked her to list what was hindering her progress, stopping her from advancing. What showed up?

Self-pity.

Fear of not finding a new job.

Fear of being thought of as incompetent.

Jealousy.

Loneliness.

And the breakthrough question: What do you gain by hanging on to these feelings?

RESULTS

Diane unhooked her leash, but not without a little grieving; she was comfortable wallowing in her emotional whirlwind, even if it contributed nothing to getting on with her life. (Remember, what we focus on is what we create.) When she realized she was gaining absolutely nothing by holding on to her feelings of anger and insecurity, it was like turning up a 'Get out of jail free' card. She realized her anger, sadness, and disappointment were all attached to a certain singular event in her life: the loss of her job. This loss did not define her but was merely a part of a chapter in her life that was now behind her—a chapter that was no longer holding her back! Her 'why' became "How can I…" and "What will I do next to…?"

How do you spell 'freedom'? Diane is going to be danger-ously dazzling at her next job interview!

SOMETHING TO CHEW ON

🐾 If you were coaching someone who needed to let go of some baggage, what action would you suggest they take?

_____

_____

🐾 What strengths do you have that will help you move in the direction you want to go?

_____

_____

🐾 How will you use them to move forward?

_____

_____

🐾 What is your ideal way of letting go of a feeling, a situation, a thought in order to lighten your load?

_____

_____

🐾 When will you begin?

_____

Tip: Remember to focus on what you can influence or control, and let go of the rest!

CHAPTER THIRTEEN:
Hitting the Wall

As I have heard, every client who is striving to create the kind of life he dreams about knows that work, discipline, frustration, sacrifice and, yes, even failure can always be a part of the picture.

Adversity is inevitable. Any goal worth striving for will be fraught with at least a few obstacles along the way or it is not worth going for. The coach likes to turn to one of his favorite writers, Napoleon Hill, author of the best-selling book *Think and Grow Rich,* for his wise advice on adversity: faced with a setback or with failing, we have two choices: become demoralized or accept to learn something from this painful situation.

Which choice would Simon make? He is a crack computer programmer with game designer ambitions. Simon wanted his newly-developed game to be an international hit and believed it was possible. He'd read about how scientists and great people had dealt with adversity. In fact, Edison was one of his heroes—he is said to have 'failed' 500 times until he finally got the light bulb to 'light' up. Simon inspired himself with popular sayings like "There is no failure, only feedback" made famous by NLP practitioners. He read all the motivational messages posted by his Facebook friends as well as the many inspirational biographies of successful people that he could find online. (I have yet to write mine!)

Simon had sent his game to many companies looking for a distributor. When he finally received a good bite from one of them, he figured he was on his way! But after much discussion and plowing ahead, the distributor changed his mind. Back to square one. And now Simon had just received his fifteenth "Thanks, but no thanks" reply from yet another distributor. His morale could not have been lower. He was beginning to have negative thoughts about his capacities and competencies as a game designer. He considered giving up. Was it all merely a pipe dream?

Edison must have been crazy.

WHY COACHING?

Floating in the inertia of self-doubt, Simon realized the only way to get out of that 'pool' and move forward was to get into action. But he just couldn't figure out how. He called the coach.

LET'S GET STARTED!

To Simon, this was the worst thing that could have happened to him. Fifteen rejections! His confidence had taken a major hit. He had done all the right things: studied in a field he loved, made goals, and had a plan of action to create a hit game. Unfortunately, after so many rejections, Simon was ready to give up. What was the use of going for something which was probably outside one's scope anyway? (That's exactly how I felt when I didn't win a ribbon at my first dog show.)

Napoleon Hill wrote that when we experience a setback, we should "look for the seed of an equivalent or greater benefit." In other words, the coach asked Simon to look for the constructive element in this situation. What could possibly be positive, but perhaps not obvious, in his current situation? Sometimes a terrible outcome can contain the 'seed' that will propel us forward, like the need to examine the situation from a different perspective, to use our imagination, to find a renewed sense of motivation, or discover what is missing in the mix.

Successful people know that adversity will create alternatives—"the equivalent or greater benefit".

People on the road to success are easily recognizable. They are resilient. They stay in action mode and try again when they meet adversity. In difficult times, they do not quit. (They go from underdog to top dog!) In fact, some people believe that failure does not exist. What *does* exist is a response to a situation that lets us know that the approach needs refining, and when trying again, we should try something new! As the saying goes, "If you haven't failed, you've never tried anything new."

We know that obstacles and failure are inevitable. And the greater the goal, the larger the obstacles. Anytime we decide to learn something new or do something innovative, it's going to involve hard work. This is what the coach suggests: start with small steps, not worrying about how long it could take to attain the desired outcome, and then refine our actions based on the results and feedback we experience. Slow and steady and always in action. It may mean leaving the comfort zone occasionally, but by using our obstacles to turn things around, as suggested by Hill, and by asking ourselves the right questions, new possibilities will present themselves.

So the coach encouraged Simon to work on asking himself an open question. He eventually changed "How can I find a distributor to pick up my game?" to "How can I distribute my game if I do not have a distributor?" With this revised focus, a new perspective on the situation appeared almost immediately. By thinking of things in a different way, our mind focuses on the possibilities instead of on the failure.

How are we going to get different results if we do not do something differently?

The coach then asked Simon to sit down and make a list of all the potential benefits he could find in this difficult situation. Just writing a list can change our focus. For Simon, this meant changing "My game is a failure," to "I want to look at ways to make my game a huge success." He turned the negative feeling of rejection into the fuelling of new ways to understand what was not working for him and an "I'm not giving up" attitude. This, most of all, allowed him to see options and the potential action he could take. Perhaps his game needed refining. Who could he turn to as a resource? Would his gamer friends test and criticize his game for him? Could he distribute the game himself through social media?

Perhaps just posting a teaser on the web would draw attention. Would crowd sourcing be a possibility? Could he turn to other designers for advice, or attend more trade shows?

RESULTS

People often collapse when faced with adversity. But by letting the obstacle generate an open question, Simon began to focus on solutions. In fact, the solution was a combination of several factors he came up with. Most importantly, though, he did not give up. He wanted badly to quit, but the coach encouraged him to stay on track—and then he got so involved in the exhilaration of moving forward that there was no way he was going to give up.

Simon used his obstacles to get where he wanted to go. He turned to his gamer friends for advice and criticism. He took on a couple of partners and found that three heads were better than one. Crowd sourcing got them on their financial feet as well as several gamer fans!

It was not without hard work and resilience, but they are now creating a spin-off of their first successful game! Shake a paw, Simon!

Edison was once again Simon's champion.

SOMETHING TO CHEW ON

🐾 Think back to a difficult moment in your life. How would you react now, knowing it's possible to find a seed of goodness in adversity—a seed that will help you move on?

🐾 What kinds of adversity are most difficult for you to handle?

_____

_____

🐾 How will you handle them going forward?

_____

_____

🐾 How can getting in touch with moments of past successes help you increase your resilience and self-confidence?

_____

_____

CHAPTER FOURTEEN:
Not Yesterday. Not Tomorrow. Now!

Do you forget someone's name as soon as you've been introduced? Do you remember what you had for supper last evening? Do you do several tasks simultaneously without really concentrating on one thing? Then you are not alone.

Because we just want to get things done, we are often unaware of the importance of being present, both to ourselves and to the world around us. We are far too busy, too worried, or depressed.

As Lao Tzu wrote over 2,500 years ago:

> If you are depressed, you are living in the past.
>
> If you are anxious, you are living in the future.
>
> If you are at peace, you are living in the present.

The coach would suggest that learning to be in the present is one of the best ways of increasing awareness. It's as simple as that. "Mindfulness" is another way of saying the same thing as is "being in the moment". Basically, these terms describe the act of being conscious of our 'selves' and the world around us *right now*—not thinking about yesterday or what we will be doing tomorrow, but simply 'being'. When we are present, we are connected; we are in the flow.

Let's take a look at Kyle's life. Kyle is a young online journalist, rigorous in his research, his fact-checking, and his passion for intelligent writing. When he came to be coached, he was still comparatively junior in his organization and was worried about his future. His record was fairly good, although he had made a couple of mistakes, as would any beginner. But Kyle didn't cut himself any slack. He obsessed over his past mistakes and was worried that they would affect his future opportunities. When he finished work at the end of the day, he turned to alcohol, sometimes a little too often, drinking alone to numb the stress. In the words of Lao Tzu, Kyle was living in the past and the future; the present moment was of no consequence. He was both depressed and anxious and it was affecting his work. He was caught in a downward spiral.

WHY COACHING?

Kyle realized that not only was he suffering, but his work and relationships were as well. He needed to come to terms with where he was at in his career and his personal life. Kyle needed to reduce his anxiety so he called the coach.

LET'S GET STARTED

Many of the themes of our previous chapters come to mind here: values, purpose, focus, fear, resilience, letting go.

Motivating the client to be in the present poses a particular challenge. So the coach used a few simple thoughts and exercises to get Kyle started on his path to peaceful awareness of the moment. (Eventually, we all develop our favourite ways of getting there.) It can start, for example, with meditation. Meditation allows us to be conscious of the moment, not daydreaming about our emails, social media postings, or past slights and future hurdles. It doesn't have to be a lengthy session; you can start with just a few minutes a day. When our thoughts wander, we just remind ourselves to come back to concentrating on our body, the moment and our breathing. Stress slips away as do thoughts from the past or concerns for the future. No worries or fears—only the pure exhilaration of being alive. Breathe in, breathe out. (I am quite the natural, if I do say so myself!)

As the coach reminded Kyle, "If you are feeling stress, it is because you are not allowing yourself to just be here. You are trying to be somewhere else at the same time. You cannot be in more than one place at a time." Being present involves just that: being where we are and not stressing over events that are happening (or have happened) elsewhere. We allow ourselves, others, and events in our lives to be what they are without judging them.

Meditating does not mean that we must empty our mind of all thoughts—it allows us to step back and get another perspective on our thoughts, to get an increased sense of clarity and focus.

Kyle worked with the coach at making a conscious effort to be aware of his breathing, and at being open and receptive to staying in the moment. This allowed him to create a space where he began to feel secure and to accept himself as he was, just Kyle, totally at ease. He slowly learned to meditate and to practice mindfulness regularly at home.

Yoga is another excellent way to be in the present. So how does this all work?

With meditation and new clarity, Kyle became aware of his negative attitudes toward himself and his work; he also recognized that he had an inclination to live in the past, a need to control his environment, and that he used pessimistic language. When he was able to release his fears tied to future employment and his regret over past mistakes, his self-acceptance soared.

Finally, the coach worked with Kyle on accepting discomfort—something none of us like. That's why we stay in our unsatisfying jobs, our predictable daily routines, and our safe relationships, otherwise referred to as our 'comfort zone'. We don't like to rock the boat. The coach began with requests for Kyle to take a few risks so he would grow used to feeling uncomfortable. It is an acquired taste (somewhat like being groomed for a dog show). But discomfort permits us to make our comfort zones even bigger—and even more comfortable. Dare to succeed!

RESULTS

With practice and time, Kyle learned to stop obsessing over past events or future possibilities. A new consciousness that events of the past were just that—over and done with—helped reduce their impact. Nor did he dwell as much on potential future problems to the detriment of the tasks at hand. When feeling stressed, he remembered to breathe consciously. Kyle discovered that staying in the 'now' was relaxing, liberating, and even exhilarating. He gained a certain sense of detachment from his thoughts. Deadlines became easier to meet and he began to get a grip on his situation. His perspective changed radically. Yesterday and tomorrow dimmed in importance. This is not to say that he was naïve about his life, or that he treated issues simplistically. As he discovered, being aware of what is happening with us, while it happens, allows us to make more conscious choices, rather than acting impulsively and emotionally. Kyle was able to make decisions more thoughtfully.

He was infused with a feeling of confidence and of being grounded. His new sense of self-esteem permitted him to enjoy the work he loved rather than considering only the past errors and how they might affect his career. Stepping out of his comfort zone, Kyle decided to ask his boss for an evaluation. He was pleasantly surprised by the results and his boss was pleased to let him know how he thought Kyle could improve.

Meditation became a way of life for him. The health benefits, such as relaxation and diminished stress, contributed greatly to his mental and spiritual well-being. His alcohol consumption was reduced to enjoyable occasions with friends. He was much happier, like waking up to a new Kyle each morning.

SOMETHING TO CHEW ON

Learning to live in the moment is a wonderful benefit of having been coached. The more we are present, the more we are alive. As they say, when we are living in the past or the future, life passes us by.

🐾 List any anxieties you may have about the future.

_____

_____

🐾 List issues from the past that continue to have an impact on your present moment.

_____

_____

🐾 What benefits do you derive from these anxieties and issues? What does living in the past or future give you?

_____

_____

🐾 What can you do to practise being in the present? What technique will you use?

_____

_____

❧ Who can support you in this venture?

_____

_____

❧ When will you begin?

_____

_____

CHAPTER FIFTEEN:
Know Thyself

One of the greatest benefits of learning to be in the moment is the emergence of increased self-awareness. Self-awareness is indeed a power. A formidable power. And, I might add, working with clients on this aspect of their lives is one of the coach's favorite steps in the entire coaching process. (A personal fave of mine too!) Self-awareness is our ability to look at how we are in the world, how we do what we do and the capacity to act upon what we learn from watching ourselves.

The coach encourages his clients to slow down long enough to consciously experience their thoughts from a different point of view and perhaps from the point of view of others as well. Think about it: being so aware of yourself that you can see yourself from a different perspective! Now that is powerful. It's almost like looking at ourselves from outside our bodies, as if in the third person. We move beyond our habitual thoughts, feelings, and emotional reactions to a new awareness, a fresh perspective that allows us to see what is stopping us from getting where we want to go!

This is a lot to digest. But I think the best way to understand self-awareness in a professional situation is to consider Anna's state of affairs. Anna is a secondary school history teacher. She had always been confident in the classroom and had enjoyed her students, for the most part. But Anna had her heart set on becoming a school principal. After fifteen years of teaching she wanted a change. When a temporary replacement position as a principal in another school district came up for grabs, she applied for and got the job. As she entered the staff room unexpectedly before leaving school one day, Anna overheard a couple of colleagues' surprised reactions as they discussed her successful nomination—but she wrote it off as jealousy.

After her ten-month period as temporary principal, the school commission announced it was planning to hold interviews to fill the position permanently. Anna felt she had impressed her new colleagues with her leadership style and was confident she had all the requisite qualifications to excel in the role—especially as she had been in place long enough to demonstrate her skills.

Anna did not get the job. Devastated, and back at her former school teaching history, she wanted to understand why she had not been chosen and what she needed to do to make sure this did not become a repeat performance.

WHY COACHING?

Anna knew she needed to look at her skills and how she was perceived by others—her colleagues and superiors. Perhaps the words she had overheard in the staff room were not merely jealous comments after all. What was missing in her style that was not allowing her to accomplish her goal? Did she, in fact, have the right stuff?

LET'S GET STARTED!

Some 3,000 years ago, Socrates, the master of self-awareness, stated that "the unexamined life is not worth living". Self-reflection and awareness can be a tall order, and often the work of a lifetime, but essential nonetheless to our happiness and well-being. Anna had already made what can be the most difficult step—accepting that something she could not put her finger on was not working for her. She realized she would have to make personal changes. But how?

The coach asked Anna to come up with a series of questions about herself that she could ask her colleagues to answer anonymously—a kind of short quiz. In the coaching world, this is called a 360 assessment: an evaluation by those surrounding us, colleagues, superiors, as well as those who may be more junior to us. The challenge in this task is to learn to see in ourselves what others may see quite clearly (and that we don't). These are called our 'blind spots'. The challenge then is to accept the feedback without being defensive. And that is definitely not easy. Obviously if we are too busy defending ourselves, we cannot hear the message.

Once our colleagues see that we are able to react openly, they understand that we can accept potential feedback now and in the future. (I remember being told as a puppy that my exuberant jumping on visitors as a welcome gesture was not seen by others in the same light. I adapted my behaviour but it was rather challenging. This set the precedent for future 'learning'.)

Systematically questioning our assumptions about ourselves keeps us in the flow, changing, growing. Remember, we are trying to slow down and examine our thoughts, feelings, and emotional reactions in order to increase our self-awareness. "Why did I react like that—so spontaneously? I hope I did not insult her."

First and foremost, we cannot act on anything that is beyond our awareness, our blind spot. If there is something about ourselves that is proving to be counter-productive, we cannot change it until we are aware of that aspect of ourselves. Sounds complicated, but it's not. If, for example, I am unaware that the others in the dog park think I am a twelve-pound weakling, how can I ever hope to lead the pack? Once I discover their impressions of me, I can act to change that. (Taking my courage in paw and standing up to that big bully in the dog run may validate my ability to lead.)

It is a question of what we learn about ourselves and our ability to change.

Secondly, once we become more self-aware, choices begin to show up. We are able to live our lives with more confidence. For example, we can now choose to be more open, more attentive at work, more positive, and to respond differently in difficult situations. We can choose with whom we would like to work, and with whom we would like to play.

The only way to increase choices is to create more self-awareness. (I like to sit with that thought for a while.)

At the coach's request, Anna circulated her questions to a few of her colleagues at both schools—questions about her leadership style, her ability to communicate, her vision, her capacity to listen and to hear opposing viewpoints, her talent to inspire. The questions were all to be answered anonymously. Bye-bye comfort zone!

RESULTS

Anna's hands trembled as she opened the evaluations; there were some positive comments and some negative, just as she had expected. Although she knew there would be criticism, what she didn't expect was the subject of the criticism. Anna was pleased to see that her ability to create a vision and to communicate it was positively received, but was surprised to see that the majority of the negative feedback dealt with her listening skills and her inability to accept opposing points of view. Not only was she perceived as unable to brook opposition, she often interrupted people as they attempted to explain their respective positions.

This was quite an eye-opener! Anna was offended, no doubt about it. But with coaching, she worked at turning the hurt into a positive experience. Now that she was conscious about her weakness as perceived by others, she knew where she had to start. (As I mentioned, we cannot work on something beyond our awareness.) The coach worked on a new objective with Anna: active listening skills. As a result, she found her colleagues slowly engaged her more often in their staff-room debates. She weighed in with caution and made sure to remind herself to not cut people off or to dismiss their opinions. Anna discovered the power of active listening and the pleasure of focusing on others. She realized that leadership often requires listening to *understand* rather than simply to *reply*.

Soon the conscious reflex to listen and not brush off the opinions of others became more of an unconscious habit—and Anna realized how much she could learn by hearing people out. By taking the time to slow down and be aware of her own thoughts, she began to take the time to slow down and listen to others as well. Self-awareness is key!

Anna is still teaching history but is finding increased support from some of her colleagues as she continues to work toward her dream of becoming a secondary school principal. She is able to ask them, face to face now, for their opinions on her skills; she listens openly to their suggestions that may just help her along the path to success.

Isn't it interesting how a little prodding from outside of ourselves opens the door to our own self-reflection and awareness? Three paws up!

SOMETHING TO CHEW ON

Self-awareness is knowing what we're good at as well as understanding that there is still a lot to learn. There is a price to pay for all this, of course: a true willingness to look at ourselves. This is the beginning of a process of transformation—and the adventure is worth it! I promise. So with this in mind:

- Take a few minutes every day at a time when you can be alone with your thoughts and quietly take a look at recent events—how you handled them, and how you would have preferred to handle them. If you feel you did well, congratulate yourself! If you are not happy with your reaction, don't be too hard on yourself. Puppy steps!

When are you most aware of your thoughts
and reactions?

_____

_____

How has a moment of new awareness changed your
thoughts or reactions/behaviour?

_____

_____

What areas in your life may require some increased self-
reflection? What assumptions could be challenged?

_____

_____

What kinds of choices have been opened up to you
now that you are becoming attuned to the power
of self-awareness?

_____

_____

CHAPTER SIXTEEN:
Wag More and Bark Less

When I am grateful, I feel like I have a hot air balloon inside of me that gets bigger and bigger until I could just float away. Sunny day, blue skies, not a cloud on the horizon—all is well with the world. Positive emotions do that to me. After my master has given me a belly rub, I am so thankful I could burst!

Have you ever noticed that it's next to impossible to feel grateful and unhappy at the same time?

Being thankful means counting our blessings—being aware of the abundance in our lives (not primarily material goods, although they can count as well). People who love us, jobs we have enjoyed, a good meal, a sunny day, a place to hang our hat (or leash)—these are things for which we can be thankful. We can even be thankful for difficult events that have led us to new insights. And what of watching our children grow, taking a walk, playing a musical instrument, enjoying a haircut? We often take many of the wonderful moments in our lives for granted.

For some of us, complaining and feeling troubled and miserable is a way of life—seeing the proverbial glass half empty instead of half full. It is focusing on what is not working or wrong instead of what is good. It is living with an attitude of scarcity rather than of abundance and fullness. Remember, as we have said, we may not be able to control the situation around us, but we can control—and change—our attitude.

So let's meet Elizabeth. She constantly moved from job to job and from relationship to relationship, looking for the perfect fit—but just couldn't seem to find it. At the beginning of a new job or relationship, she would think she was at last satisfied, but then would get restless and begin to look for greener pastures once again. There was always something that didn't 'work'. She had tried her hand at sales, teaching, and product development. Elizabeth was still looking but couldn't seem to find what she was looking for. She was fairly comfortable financially and had few material needs, but experienced feelings of emptiness. She acknowledged that her glass was half empty.

WHY COACHING?

Elizabeth realized her pattern was leading nowhere. She had no joy in her life and could not seem to find value in much that she had accomplished. She walked around with a dark cloud over her head.

LET'S GET STARTED

One of the breakthroughs my master's clients experience is a quantum shift in their thinking. Changing our thinking is another way of getting into action. And as we know by now, coaching is about getting into action—on many levels.

Elizabeth was so busy looking for something new and better that she was not aware of the abundance in her life. Like many, she took for granted the good that was already a part of her world. Working with Elizabeth to increase her awareness of and gratitude for what she had, the coach began with a few simple exercises. First he asked her to imagine what it would be like to lose some of the things she currently took for granted: her love of singing, her ability to jog, her relationship with her best friend since grade three, among others. Yikes! Then, if she were to have these pleasures returned to her one by one, how would she feel? The words "thankful" and "grateful" immediately leapt to mind. (Sometimes we never know what we have until it's gone.)

Another exercise that the coach often suggests to his clients is the writing of a thankfulness diary. Each day, Elizabeth recorded everything for which she was grateful. This was a revelation to her. She was overwhelmed with how much abundance surrounded her when she took the time to look and appreciate it.

The coach also asked her a couple of his favorite powerful questions: "What is working presently in your life?" and

"What do you have to be grateful for, right now?" These questions open the way to looking at all that is positive in our lives, the options, the possibilities. They change the negative lens for a more positive one and help us focus on what is good and 'perfect' in our world.

Elizabeth was surprised that her answers to the coach's questions were not as short as she thought they would be.

RESULTS

Listing what she was thankful for allowed Elizabeth to reframe how she saw herself. She realized how much abundance existed right under her nose. Her perspective changed; her glass was indeed more than half full. Looking at her situation with a positive reframed attitude, she began to find a new way of seeing the events in her life. As she became more aware of what she actually had, Elizabeth understood that her constant search for the 'perfect fit' was totally unnecessary. She was already surrounded by perfect abundance. She had wonderful parents; she enjoyed singing in a choir; her health was good and she was fit enough not only to jog but also to play a pretty mean game of squash. Her perspective on her career and relationships began to change as she allowed herself to appreciate life more fully.

Elizabeth found herself creating positive actions that were empowering both for herself and for others. She relaxed and began to feel joy and experience success. People were drawn to this new Elizabeth and enjoyed spending time with her. She started to catch herself when she complained about something.

Being grateful for someone or something is positive and constructive. Modern science is proving that developing a 'gratefulness attitude' is good for our health and general well-being. Thankful thoughts and feelings generate smiles, optimism, and solutions. Who could not help but be drawn to someone who is so "rich"?

SOMETHING TO CHEW ON

Numerous studies in positive psychology point to the fact that grateful people are more likely to be happier and experience less stress. Focusing on what we have sows the seeds of success.

🐾 Make a list of all the things and events and people that make your life rich.

_____

_____

_____

_____

🐾 What is presently working in your life?

_____

_____

_____

_____

🐾 What is good about your present situation?

_____

_____

_____

_____

CHAPTER SEVENTEEN:
The Good Life

So, here we are, at the final chapter of this great adventure. Ultimately, the purpose of coaching is to help everyone arrive at a more satisfying, successful and happy existence. Happiness! We each have our unique personal definition of happiness. Perhaps the coach and I have been beneficial to you in your quest. We sincerely hope this is true. (I hope your inner hot air balloon is full!)

As we mentioned at the very beginning of the book, my master, the coach, helps people make the leap from where they are now to where they want to be. He helps them discover what is missing and then works with them to design the steps that will close the gap separating them from where they are at the moment and their desired destination. This takes the time that it takes and there is excitement to be savoured in the self-revelations and accomplishments as the gap closes. It is not a race, it's a process—and most clients eventually reach their goals related to relationships, finances, career, spirituality, or personal growth and health.

But there are also goals which take us to another level on this journey. These goals spring from our core values and purpose in life. During the coaching process, these deeper elements may rise to the surface. Clients may ask more philosophical, psychological, or even spiritual questions: "Who am I really? What is my existence all about? Where am I headed? What will I contribute to the world?" These concerns are also reflected in an increasing general interest in yoga, meditation, mindfulness training, spirituality and philosophy.

You may have experienced these same feelings as you worked through your something-to-chew-on exercises.

As long as humans (and some four-legged creatures!) have walked the Earth, we have taken many different paths in our search for meaning and true happiness. This is where the coaching process can have a powerful impact as clients work toward getting in touch with the bigger picture. These are not 'having' or 'doing' goals, but a desire on the part of the client to delve more deeply within to uncover the true direction for their 'being'. Of course, accomplishing goals makes us happy, but finding meaning in what we see as our purpose in life goes well beyond our 'to-do' list. This is a significant breakthrough for many of those who have been through the coaching process.

Over the years, psychologists have identified many pathways to happiness—enjoyment, commitment, and meaning are just a few. To this I would add loving, being loved, and giving to others. (We canines specialize in unconditional love.) A coach will help clients spend as much time as possible on realizing what will really make them happy. Think back to Elizabeth who discovered the pleasure of her abundance, or Simon who found great happiness in his resilience and success as a game designer, and Roger who committed to signing up for his first half marathon. And what of Melissa, the IT project manager who developed an entirely new work-life balance? And finally, Andrea, whose new understanding of responsibility gave her a meaningful reason for going to work each day. All of these coaching experiences were transformational, for it is in the 'being' that happiness, commitment, and meaning are found.

One thing all clients will experience in coaching is the understanding that happiness is not primarily created by events in their environment, but by their own particular response to these events. Indeed, happiness is a state of mind depending on our values, vision, and purpose in life. In this book, we have followed the coaching process by exploring our values and deeper motives, developing resiliency, courage, and optimism. We have looked at becoming responsible, learning to accept whatever happens, while making a conscious effort to live in the present. We have delved into the idea of becoming more self-aware, and of discovering gratitude. All of these steps open the door to contentment, personal success, and true happiness.

Each client's journey is personal and unique. Working with a coach helps us discover the internal resources and tools that will encourage us as we move toward our destination. Some of us will find a greater work-life balance and a sense of empowerment; others will develop increased capacity for self-reflection and empathy. On the professional level, some clients will improve their ability to market themselves, to network, and to use their new goal-setting abilities to help them succeed.

Finally, I would like to draw your attention to what I feel is one of the greatest benefits of the coaching experience: mental flexibility. Partnering with a coach allows us to develop responses to events that are no longer impulsive reactions based on limiting beliefs (remember them?). We have a new awareness. We have acquired new ways of reacting to internal and external events and can adjust our behaviour accordingly. We have acquired the ability to relativize. We can choose to decide what meaning we want to give to our lives. It's all up to us!

At the outset of this book, we mentioned how the importance of personal values and a sense of mission are essential to us all—how it is important to align our life and actions with our values and purpose. You now know the secret to living the good life! Ultimately, happiness is not something we find; it is something we choose and create. With the help of a coach, clients explore and work on developing their own winning conditions. The ultimate goal is more than succeeding in a job—it's succeeding in our lives!

SOMETHING TO CHEW ON

What difference do you want to make in this lifetime?

🐾 What does "The purpose of life is to have a purpose" now mean to you?

_____

_____

🐾 What does living your truth and being your self really mean to you?

_____

_____

🐾 What makes you happy? How do you make others happy?

_____

_____

🐾 What are you going to do about it? When?

_____

_____

Choose to have fun!
Spread the joy!
Rub someone behind the ear!

NOTES

NOTES

NOTES

CPSIA information can be obtained
at www.ICGtesting.com
Printed in the USA
LVOW04s0720281115

464483LV00033B/453/P